Fundamentals to Catching up to Crypto

Guide to bitcoin and new digital Economy

Epris E. Ezekiel

Contents

Introduction to the Digital Economy

In this book, we will embark on an exciting journey to explore the world of cryptocurrencies and the underlying technology that powers them – blockchain. This chapter will provide an overview of the digital economy, the rise of cryptocurrencies, and their importance in reshaping our financial landscape.

Chapter 1: The Digital Revolution

One of the major areas of change brought about by the digital revolution has been the way we manage our money. The digital revolution has had a profound impact on many facets of our life. Money has evolved throughout history, from simple bartering systems to the sophisticated financial systems we use today. A completely new paradigm for exchanging value in the digital era has also been established by the emergence of cryptocurrencies.

Money's Evolution

The history of money as a means of transaction is incredibly long and fascinating. Simple bartering systems, where products and services were transferred directly between people, formed the foundation of early human society. However, bartering had intrinsic drawbacks, such as the "double coincidence of wants" issue, which required both parties to simultaneously desire what the other was providing.

Humans began adopting commodity money to get over these restrictions, using things like shells, salt, precious metals (like gold and silver), or even livestock as a standardized medium of exchange. These goods had intrinsic worth that was well-known in their respective civilizations.

Carrying heavy and unwieldy goods for commerce became impossible as societies developed and expanded. As a result, paper notes or certificates representing claims on reserves of commodities like gold or silver began to emerge. These notes made trade more convenient and portable on a bigger scale.

The introduction of fiat money systems marked the next significant advancement in the development of money. According to this theory, the value of money was determined by how much people trusted the institution that issued it, which was often the government or a central bank. Fiat currencies rely on the government's ability to manage their supply and preserve stability rather than being backed by any tangible assets.

How Cryptocurrencies Began

Another important turning point in the development of money was the introduction of the Internet in the latter part of the 20th century. The internet revolutionized communication, trade, and finance by enabling the digital flow of information around the world.

The first decentralized cryptocurrency, Bitcoin, was launched to the world in 2009 by an unidentified individual or group that went by the pseudonym Satoshi Nakamoto. Blockchain, the technology that underpins Bitcoin, offered a safe and open method of keeping track of transactions without the need for a central authority. Because cryptocurrencies are decentralized, there is no longer a requirement for financial transactions to go via intermediaries like banks.

The invention of Bitcoin spawned a wave of innovation that resulted in the creation of countless more cryptocurrencies, often known as altcoins. Each cryptocurrency runs on its own blockchain and fulfills a variety of functions, from enabling quick and affordable international payments to enabling decentralized apps (Dapps) and smart contract.

Chapter 2: Benefits of Using Digital Currencies

• Financial Inclusion

Digital currencies, especially cryptocurrencies, have the potential to increase financial inclusion, which is one of their most important benefits. Large populations around the world often lack access to standard banking services owing to inadequate infrastructure, documentation, or credit histories. Due to their availability on smartphones and the internet, digital currencies can enable underbanked and unbanked communities to engage in the global economy.

• Confidentiality and security

Cryptographic methods are used by cryptocurrencies to secure transactions and shield users' identities. On immutable public ledgers (blockchains), which are transparent and available for audit by anyone, transactions are recorded. Users may independently confirm the validity of transactions thanks to this transparency, which promotes confidence. Additionally, compared to conventional centralized systems, cryptocurrencies are less vulnerable to fraud and hacking due to their decentralized nature.

- ## **Faster cross-border payments and lower transaction fees**

Particularly for international transactions, traditional financial systems frequently charge large transaction fees. As there is no need for intermediaries like banks, cryptocurrencies, on the other hand, often have lower fees. Additionally, regardless of distance, cross-border bitcoin transactions can happen relatively instantly, drastically cutting down the time it takes to settle international payments.

- ## **Borderless**

The use of cryptocurrencies allows for seamless international trade across boundaries. Currency conversions and settlement times are frequent problems for traditional banking systems, which causes delays and extra costs. By enabling smooth international trade and financial transactions, digital currencies provide a borderless solution.

• Ownership and Financial Sovereignty

Individuals rely on financial organizations to hold and manage their funds under traditional banking systems. However, this compromises the person's control over their finances because in some circumstances, banks may apply limitations or even freeze accounts. Because they are decentralized and dependent on cryptographic keys, cryptocurrencies give consumers total control over their money. Individuals are able to act as their own custodians and keep ownership of their possessions thanks to this financial independence.

Chapter 3: Blockchain Technology: The Backbone of Crypto

Blockchain technology has become a powerful force in the last ten years, revolutionizing several industries and setting the stage for the advent of cryptocurrencies. Blockchain is fundamentally a distributed and decentralized ledger technology that makes it possible to record transactions in a secure and open manner. Because it serves as the foundation for the functionality of cryptocurrencies, this technology has come to be synonymous with them.

Understanding Blockchain Technology

Blockchain is a sequence of interconnected blocks that serves as a digital ledger for transactions. Once a block is finished, it is added to the chain, creating an immutable and chronological list of transaction records. Each block contains a list of transactions. Blockchain is a decentralized technology, which means that there is no single central authority in charge of it; rather, it is maintained by a network of computers (called nodes) located all over the world.

The cryptographic methods and consensus procedures used by blockchain contribute to its security and dependability. Blockchains based on Proof of Work, like Bitcoin, or Proof of Stake, like Ethereum, use network nodes to verify transactions and group them into blocks. This process is known as mining. Due to the computing effort needed and the distributed structure of the network, modifying any information in earlier blocks becomes very difficult after a block is added to the chain.

Blockchain's Function in Cryptocurrencies

A key component of cryptocurrencies is blockchain technology, which addresses the long-standing issue of double spending in virtual currency. There is a possibility that a user could use the same digital currency unit more than once in a typical digital payment system, such as online banking. On the other hand, a blockchain-based system eliminates this risk thanks to the consensus process and transactional order.

A bitcoin transaction is broadcast to the network when it is started by a user. The network nodes then contend with one another to approve and include this transaction in a block. When all nodes agree, the block is added to the chain and the transaction is regarded as confirmed. The cryptocurrency recipient can now be convinced that the digital asset they received is legitimate and hasn't been used elsewhere.

Additionally, because of the decentralized nature of blockchain technology, cryptocurrencies are free from centralized control. Cryptocurrencies work on a peer-to-peer network, unlike conventional fiat currencies that are produced and controlled by governments, offering individuals more power over their money and financial activities.

Chapter 4: Benefits of Blockchain in the Crypto

- **Security:** Blockchain is extremely secure against fraud and hacker attempts due to its immutability and cryptographic capabilities. A transaction becomes very difficult to change or manipulate once it is recorded on the blockchain, increasing the overall security of the crypto ecosystem.

- **Transparency:** Every transaction made on the blockchain is open to the public and transparent. Since anybody can see a cryptocurrency's whole transaction history, the system is more trustworthy and accountable.

- **Decentralization:** Because blockchain is decentralized, there is no single point of failure, which strengthens and stabilizes the network. This feature also guards against censorship and central authority control, which is consistent with the fundamental ideas behind cryptocurrencies.

- **Speed and Efficiency:** Peer-to-peer transactions using blockchain-based cryptocurrencies are faster and more efficient, even across different continents, than those using traditional banking systems, which might take several days.

- **Lower Costs:** Compared to traditional financial systems, blockchain transactions have much lower transaction fees due to the lack of intermediaries, making them more affordable for users.

Challenges and Upcoming Changes

Although blockchain technology has significantly benefited the cryptocurrency industry, there are some drawbacks as well. As the volume of transactions on some blockchains increases exponentially, scalability is a serious worry. Solutions including layer-two protocols, sharding, and enhanced consensus methods are being used to try to solve this problem.

Concerns about the environment have also been expressed in relation to the energy usage of Proof of Work blockchains. Many projects are switching to more energy-efficient consensus mechanisms, including Proof of Stake, in response.

Blockchain technology is anticipated to become more prevalent outside of cryptocurrencies in the future. Supply chain management, voting procedures, identity verification, decentralized finance (DeFi), and many other things could be used with it. The field's continual research and development are opening the road for cutting-edge application cases, further solidifying blockchain's place as a transformational technology.

Chapter 5: Understanding Bitcoin

In this chapter, we will delve into the foundational cryptocurrency, Bitcoin. Understanding Bitcoin is crucial as it laid the groundwork for many other digital assets and sparked a financial revolution. We will explore its history and how it works.

The Enigmatic Creator: Satoshi Nakamoto

The world of banking and online transactions has undergone a change thanks to Bitcoin, the first and best-known cryptocurrency. Since it was first introduced in 2009, Satoshi Nakamoto, the creator who goes by the pseudonym, has left little information regarding their real identity.

On a cryptography email list in October 2008, a person or group going by the alias Satoshi Nakamoto posted a whitepaper titled "Bitcoin: A Peer-to-Peer Electronic Cash System" on the internet. This ground-breaking paper presented a decentralized digital currency that relied on cryptographic evidence rather than faith in a central authority, outlining the fundamental ideas and technology underpinning Bitcoin.

The identity of Satoshi Nakamoto's real self has remained a closely-guarded secret despite the revolutionary idea. No concrete proof of the identity of the person(s) behind the moniker has come to light as of yet. Although numerous hypotheses and examinations have been made, none have successfully identified the creator. Before he vanished from view in 2010, Nakamoto connected with early Bitcoin developers and consumers via email and online forums.

Despite the mystery surrounding Nakamoto's identity, their invention has had a significant impact on the technology and financial world. A digital revolution in banking and technology was sparked by the development of Bitcoin, which paved the way for a variety of alternative cryptocurrencies.

How Bitcoin Operates: A Simple Description

Blockchain technology is used by Bitcoin's decentralized network to facilitate safe and transparent transactions without the use of middlemen like banks. An overview of Bitcoin's operation is provided below:

• Transactions

A user creates a digital message with the recipient's address, the desired amount, and a private key signature when they start a Bitcoin transaction. The entire network is then informed of this message.

• Verification

The transaction message is added to a pool of pending transactions, where miners select it for confirmation. Proof of Work (PoW) is a technique used by network users known as "miners" to solve challenging mathematical puzzles.

- **Mining and Consensus**

The security and consensus mechanism of Bitcoin depend on mining. The first miner to crack the code adds the following block of transactions to the blockchain. Miners compete to crack the code. It is challenging to change a block's contents after it has been inserted, guaranteeing the ledger's immutability.

Chapter 6: Mining and Blockchain

Mining Method

The Bitcoin network's backbone, mining provides a number of functions. It creates fresh bitcoins into circulation in addition to validating transactions. Newly created bitcoins and transaction fees paid by users for quicker transaction processing are given to miners as payment for their work.

The Miners' Role

Miners compete by using processing power to solve challenging mathematical riddles. This procedure is competitive and uses a lot of energy because it needs a lot of computer resources. In order to ensure that new blocks are added roughly every ten minutes and maintain a constant transaction rate, the difficulty of the puzzles rises as more miners join the network.

Concerns about Mining Centralization

Concerns regarding the concentration of mining power have grown over time. Large mining pools have formed, concentrating processing capacity as mining becomes more competitive and resource-intensive. Because of this concentration of strength, there is a risk of malevolent actors seizing control of the majority of the network's mining power and influencing transactions, or "51 percent" assaults.

Getting Started

As a decentralized digital money, Bitcoin, the first and best-known cryptocurrency, has achieved enormous appeal. Without the need of conventional financial intermediaries like banks, it enables users to send and receive transactions through the internet.

Opening a Bitcoin Wallet

You'll need a digital wallet to securely store and manage your currency before you can purchase Bitcoin. An application or piece of software called a cryptocurrency wallet lets you transmit, receive, and store digital assets. There are various wallet varieties, each with benefits and drawbacks:

Online wallets are web-based wallets that can be accessed using a web browser. They are practical but may be less secure because your private keys—which are needed to access your funds—are kept on a server owned by a third party.

- **Mobile wallets:** These are applications created for tablets and smartphones that provide you the freedom to manage your Bitcoin while you're on the go. Although they are generally safe, you should take security measures to guard against loss or illegal access to your device.

- **Desktop wallets:** Installed on your PC, desktop wallets provide greater security compared to online wallets because you retain ownership of your private keys. Update your computer frequently, and secure it with antivirus software and strong passwords.

- **Hardware wallets:** Physical objects that physically hold your private keys offline are among the choices that are thought to be the most secure. Online dangers like viruses and hacking attempts are unaffected by them.

Simple printed QR codes or paper records of your private keys make up paper wallets. The physical document must be handled carefully and kept in a secure location despite being secure.

Pick a wallet based on your requirements and level of risk tolerance. Popular wallets include Ledger Nano S (hardware), Exodus (desktop and mobile), and Coinbase (internet).

Purchasing Bitcoin

The next step after creating a wallet is to purchase Bitcoin. There are several ways to buy Bitcoin, and the alternatives could vary depending on where you are. These are the most typical methods:

- **Cryptocurrency Exchanges:** These online marketplaces let you purchase Bitcoin using conventional fiat currencies (such as USD, EUR, etc.). The popular exchanges Coinbase, Binance, Kraken, and Bitstamp are just a few examples. You must set up an account, go through identity verification (KYC), and link your bank account or credit/debit card to your account in order to utilize an exchange.

- **Bitcoin ATMs:** You can insert cash into some cities' Bitcoin ATMs to obtain Bitcoins instantly to your wallet. For larger transactions, some ATMs could demand identity verification.

- **Peer-to-Peer (P2P) Platforms:** You may acquire bitcoin using a variety of payment options thanks to these platforms' direct connections between buyers and sellers. Paxful and Local Bitcoins are two examples. When interacting with people on P2P sites, use cautious and undertake extensive investigation.

Advanced investors may want to checkout Bitcoin futures and derivatives on cryptocurrency exchanges like BitMEX or Binance Futures. These products carry a higher level of risk and are better suited for seasoned traders.

Keeping and Protecting Your Bitcoin

To avoid theft or financial loss, it's essential to store Bitcoin safely after obtaining it. The following are crucial pointers for safe storage:

If your gadget is lost or destroyed, you can still access your money by regularly backing up your wallet's private keys or seed phrase.

Use two-factor authentication (2FA) to add an extra degree of security to your exchange and wallet accounts.

- ❖ **Phishing Scams to Avoid:** Be wary of phishing scams that use emails or websites that pretend to be reputable businesses. Verify URLs twice and never divulge your private keys or passwords.

❖ **Software Updates:** Updating the software on your device and wallet will help you stay safe against vulnerabilities.

❖ **Diversify Your Holdings:** To reduce risk, think about spreading out your investments over various wallets and cryptocurrencies.

Bitcoin's Monetary Policy: The Halving

1. Limited Supply by Halving

The monetary system of Bitcoin is intended to resemble the rarity of precious metals like gold. Since there are only 21 million bitcoins available, it is a deflationary currency. With time, a mechanism known as "Halving" causes the rate at which new bitcoins are issued to be in circulation to slow down.

2. The Process of Halving

The number of bitcoins mined per block is cut in half about every four years. After the first halving in 2012, the reward for miners dropped to 25 bitcoins each block from the initial 50 bitcoins per block. The reward was further decreased to 12.5 bitcoins per block at the second halving in 2016.

3. The Effects of Halving

The Halving has a number of effects. First of all, it increases scarcity, which historically has increased the value of Bitcoin. Second, it has an impact on the rewards for miners, potentially resulting in lower profitability for some miners, which can have an impact on mining centralization.

Chapter 7: Investing in Cryptocurrencies

In recent years, the world of cryptocurrencies has attracted a great deal of attention and investment interest. Many investors have been lured to the emergence of digital assets like Bitcoin, Ethereum, and others because of the possibility for significant gains in this emerging and dynamic market. Significant opportunities do, however, often come with significant hazards.

Understanding Crypto Market Volatility

The tremendous volatility of the bitcoin market is one of its distinguishing features. Prices of digital assets can fluctuate dramatically and quickly, resulting in large gains or losses in a short amount of time. Numerous elements, including market mood, governmental changes, technical improvements, and macroeconomic events, have an impact on this volatility.

Investors need to be cautious and take a long-term view

in order to deal with the volatility in the crypto markets. A crucial risk-reduction method is diversification. Investors may be able to lessen the effects of a downturn in one industry or asset by spreading their assets across a variety of cryptocurrencies, businesses, and geographical locations. Additionally, keeping a disciplined attitude during market turmoil can be facilitated by having defined investment goals and following a well-thought-out investment plan. **Wallets and security precautions**

Securing your cryptocurrency should be your top priority when investing. Cryptocurrencies, unlike conventional financial systems, rely on decentralized networks and cryptographic keys to operate. In order to properly preserve their digital assets, investors must be aware of the many types of wallets that are available as well as the security measures.

a) **Wallet varieties**:

- Hardware wallets: By storing private keys offline, these tangible gadgets are less vulnerable to online threats and hacker efforts.

- **Software wallets:** Programs or applications that can be downloaded and installed on computers, smartphones, or other gadgets. While useful, if not properly secured, they are more susceptible to cyberattacks.

- **Paper wallets:** Offline storage of a printed copy of the public and private keys. Although they add an additional degree of security, they are readily broken or lost.

b) Security precautions

- **Strong Passwords:** Avoid using combinations that are simple to guess and instead use singular, complicated passwords to access your wallet.

Enable two-factor authentication (2FA) whenever you can to strengthen the security of your accounts.

Update your wallet software and programs frequently to include the most recent security fixes.

- **Cold Storage:** Keep the majority of your cryptocurrency holdings offline and cut off from the internet by storing them in hardware or paper wallets.

- **Backup:** To prevent possible data loss, regularly backup the information on your wallet.

- **Phishing Alert:** Be wary of phony emails, websites, or messages that try to deceive you into divulging personal information.

Other Suggestions for Responsible and Safe Investing

Take the time to educate yourself on how Bitcoin and the larger cryptocurrency market operate. You'll be better able to make selections if you are knowledgeable.

Because cryptocurrency markets can be very volatile, only invest money that you can afford to lose. Do not invest money you cannot afford to lose without jeopardizing your ability to meet your basic necessities.

- **Avoid FOMO and Panic:** When prices fluctuate, resist the need to panic or feel like you're missing out. Keep an extended perspective.

Consider utilizing a dollar-cost averaging technique, in which you make a fixed investment at predetermined periods to lessen the impact of price fluctuation.

- **Stay Current:** Stay up to date on advancements in the bitcoin industry, changes to regulations, and security procedures

Avoiding Fraud and Recognizing Scams

The amount of frauds and fraudulent operations in the cryptocurrency field has increased along with the popularity of cryptocurrencies. Investors must be aware of such frauds and take the appropriate security measures to safeguard their capital.

- Ponzi schemes, which pay returns to earlier investors using the capital of new investors, are one type of investment plan in which scammers may offer huge returns on investments.

- Initial Coin Offerings (ICOs) are occasions for new cryptocurrencies to raise money. Fraudulent ICOs may make exaggerated returns promises or straight-up steal money without keeping their word.

- Pump-and-Dump Schemes: In these, the price of a cryptocurrency is artificially inflated using false information, and then the asset is sold off at its highest value, leaving other investors with substantial losses.

- Social engineering: Scammers may try to influence people via social media or other platforms in order to get private keys or sensitive data.

In order to protect yourself from fraud and scams, investors should:

- Before investing in a cryptocurrency, do extensive research on the projects and teams.

- Be wary of promises that sound unrealistically excellent to be true.

- Don't divulge private information to unreliable sources.

- Verify the validity of URLs and email addresses twice.

- Before making any investing decisions, seek guidance from reliable sources and financial professionals.

Analyzing Fundamentals and Cryptocurrencies for Investment

Understanding fundamental analysis is essential for making wise investing choices in the quickly changing world of cryptocurrencies. Although the cryptocurrency industry is infamous for its volatility, using a thorough strategy to evaluate a cryptocurrency's value and prospects can help investors cut through the clutter and spot interesting opportunities. We will examine the key elements of fundamental analysis, with a particular emphasis on assessing a cryptocurrency's use case, scrutinizing the development teams and community, and taking market movements and sentiment into account.

Cryptocurrency's Use Case

The use case of a cryptocurrency is the issue it seeks to address or the function it performs inside the blockchain ecosystem. The long-term success and adoption of a cryptocurrency depend critically on a compelling use case. Here are some important aspects to take into account when assessing the use case for a cryptocurrency:

- Does the cryptocurrency have any other uses besides serving as a speculative asset? Look for initiatives that provide answers for current issues, such as supply chain management, identity verification, decentralized applications (Dapps), or decentralized finance (DeFi) platforms.

- Uniqueness: What distinguishes the cryptocurrency from its rivals? In a crowded market, a project might stand out from the competition with a distinctive selling proposition, increasing acceptance and possibly raising the project's price.

- Market Demand: Does the use case for the cryptocurrency have any real demand? Users and investors are more likely to become interested in a project that targets sizable markets or sectors with major pain issues.

- Examine the degree of adoption the cryptocurrency has attained and any relationships it may have made with reputable organizations or businesses. Successful collaborations can bolster the project's credibility and pave the way for wider acceptance.

- Scalability and underlying technology: Examine the scalability of the underlying blockchain technology. A project is more likely to meet rising demand and usage if it can process many transactions per second and has plans for future scaling.

Evaluation of Community and Development Teams

A solid and competent development staff stands behind every fruitful cryptocurrency project. The project's conception and execution are greatly influenced by the team's knowledge, experience, and commitment. Following are some things to take into account when assessing the development team and community:

- **Experience and qualifications:** Look into the history of the main team members. Do they possess relevant expertise in the creation of blockchains, cryptography, or other related areas? Verify their prior endeavors and contributions to the blockchain community.

- **Transparency:** Look for initiatives that keep information about team members open and regularly update stakeholders on their status. Transparency issues may be cause for concern.

- **GitHub Activity:** To determine the level of activity, look at the project's GitHub repository. A good quantity of updates, contributions, and commits indicates a dynamic development process.

- **Community Engagement:** For a cryptocurrency project, a vibrant and active community is encouraging. Search for active social media platforms, forums, and neighborhood-based projects. Adoption can be sparked by community support, which will also help the project succeed.

- Examine the token distribution to make sure it is equitable and isn't concentrated among a select few holders. Decentralization and market manipulation can both be avoided with properly dispersed tokens.

Taking Market Trends and Sentiment into Account

To make wise investment choices, it is crucial to take into account larger market trends and mood in addition to the individual characteristics of a bitcoin project. Here are some things to consider:

- **Market Capitalization and Trading Volume:** Examine the market capitalization and trading volume of the coin. Projects with more market capitalization and liquidity typically have higher levels of stability and draw institutional interest.

- **Price Performance in the Past and Volatility:** Research the cryptocurrency's past price performance to determine its volatility. High volatility can be harmful for **long-term investors** but can offer chances for traders.

- Observe the regulatory trends in the bitcoin industry, both internationally and in particular locations. The mood of the market and the viability of a project can both be significantly impacted by regulatory changes.

- **Media Coverage and Social Attitude**: Keep an eye on the cryptocurrency's media coverage and social attitude. Detrimental publicity can have detrimental impacts, while positive news and community support can increase the project's reputation and price.

- **Market Cycle:** Identify the market cycle's stage. Markets for cryptocurrencies frequently experience boom and bust cycles. Setting reasonable expectations for prospective returns might be aided by being aware of where the market is in its cycle.

- Consider macroeconomic elements including interest rates, inflation, and geopolitical developments. These may have an impact on investors' risk tolerance and the bitcoin market.

Chapter 8: Altcoins

As a decentralized digital currency that has the capacity to upend established financial systems, Bitcoin's introduction in 2009 changed the financial landscape. Numerous other cryptocurrencies, often known as "altcoins," have entered the market in the wake of Bitcoin's triumph. Within the larger blockchain and cryptocurrency ecosystem, altcoins are created to serve specific use cases and niche markets while providing distinctive features, upgrades, or alternatives to Bitcoin.

How do Altcoins work?

The word "altcoins," which stands for "alternative coins," refers to all cryptocurrencies besides Bitcoin. They cover a broad spectrum of digital assets, each with unique characteristics and value propositions. These coins, which frequently aim to overcome perceived constraints or flaws in Bitcoin's design, are created using various distributed ledger or blockchain technology.

Alternate currency types include:

a. **Smart Contract Platforms:** Some alternative currencies, like as Ethereum, Cardano, and Solana, act as platforms for smart contracts. They make it possible for programmers to design and distribute programmable smart contract-capable decentralized applications (Dapps). These platforms enable a wide range of use cases, including supply chain management, decentralized finance (DeFi), and non-fungible tokens (NFTs).

b. **Privacy Coins:** Cryptocurrencies that put a strong emphasis on transaction privacy and anonymity include Dash, Monero, and Zcash. They use sophisticated encryption methods to conceal transactional information and safeguard user identities.

c. **Payment Coins:** Litecoin, Bitcoin Cash, and Ripple were created as alternatives to Bitcoin in order to be more effective payment methods. They frequently provide reduced rates, quicker transaction speeds, or improved scalability to meet bigger transaction volumes.

d. **Stablecoins:** Stablecoins are digital currencies that are linked to reliable assets like commodities or fiat money, such Tether, USD Coin, and DAI. They seek to preserve a constant value, which qualifies them for a variety of uses, including hedging against market volatility and permitting simple conversion into conventional currencies.

The following are some reasons why altcoins are important:

a. **Innovation and Experimentation:** Altcoins promote ongoing innovation and experimentation in the cryptocurrency industry. Each altcoin provides fresh technological developments that might someday find their way into Bitcoin itself or other projects.

b. **Diversification:** A wide variety of altcoins benefits investors and traders by enabling them to diversify their cryptocurrency portfolios. Different altcoins could see distinctive price fluctuations, giving traders chances to benefit under diverse market circumstances.

c. **Addressing Limitations:** Alternate cryptocurrencies make an effort to solve Bitcoin's alleged shortcomings in terms of scalability, privacy, and adaptability. The bitcoin ecosystem is improved and grows as a result of this competition.

Risks and Challenges:

a. The cryptocurrency market, including that for altcoins, is notoriously unstable. Prices can change drastically in a short amount of time, posing dangers to investors.

b. **Lack of Regulation:** The legal framework surrounding cryptocurrency is always changing. Similar to other digital assets, altcoins may be subject to ambiguous regulatory frameworks in different countries, which may have an impact on their development and uptake.

c. **Security Issues:** Bitcoin, which has the advantage of being the first and most extensively used cryptocurrency, may have higher levels of security and robustness than altcoins.

d. **Rivalry and Survival:** The market for alternative currencies is saturated with fierce rivalry. Many cryptocurrencies struggle to gain traction or stay relevant, which results in high failure rates.

Conclusion

Armed with the knowledge gained from this book, you are now equipped to navigate the exciting world of cryptocurrencies and blockchain technology confidently. Remember, the digital economy is continually evolving, so stay curious, keep learning, and embrace the opportunities that lie ahead in this transformative era. Happy investing and exploring the crypto frontier!

www.ingramcontent.com/pod-product-compliance
Lightning Source LLC
Chambersburg PA
CBHW051359250726
48656CB00006B/2170